TH[...]STS
OF [...]HY

A Statement of Findings and Recommendations

≋ ≋ ≋ ≋ ≋ ≋ ≋ ≋

These Findings and Recommendations
have been prepared by

MARY EBERSTADT

Research Fellow of the Hoover Institution

———— and ————

MARY ANNE LAYDEN

Director of the Sexual Trauma and Psychopathology Program
Center for Cognitive Therapy
Department of Psychiatry
University of Pennsylvania

THE WITHERSPOON INSTITUTE
PRINCETON, NEW JERSEY

▲

‹ STI ›

▼

Social Trends Institute
NEW YORK · BARCELONA

Published in the United States of America by the Witherspoon Institute
16 Stockton Street, Princeton, New Jersey 08540

Library of Congress Control Number: 2010920646

ISBN: 9780981491127

Printed in the United States of America

Footnoted text on page 19 taken from "Acquiring Tastes and Loves," from *The Brain That Changes Itself: Stories of Personal Triumph from the Frontiers of Brain Science*, by Norman Doidge, copyright ©2007 by Norman Doidge, used by permission of Viking Penguin, a division of Penguin Group (USA) Inc.

Cover design and layout by Design4 Marketing Communications
Printing by Thomson-Shore

EXECUTIVE SUMMARY

SINCE THE BEGINNING OF THE INTERNET AGE, pornography has been consumed in greater quantities than ever before in human history, and its content has grown more graphic. Recent research suggests that pornography consumption—especially consumption of a more hard-core or violent sort— has negative effects on individuals and society. More studies are necessary, but a growing body of research strongly suggests that for some users pornography can be psychologically addictive, and can negatively affect the quality of interpersonal relationships, sexual health and performance, and social expectations about sexual behavior. Widespread pornography consumption appears to pose a serious challenge to public health and to personal and familial well-being. With concerted action from legislators, the therapeutic community, educators, policymakers, and responsible corporate leaders, however, some of the negative effects of pornography consumption can be combated.

The Witherspoon Institute is grateful to the SOCIAL TRENDS INSTITUTE, the CASTER FAMILY TRUST, and the STUART FAMILY FOUNDATION for making this project possible.

*Please note that this report contains graphic language
to convey the reality of contemporary pornography and its
impact on men, women, and children.*

TABLE OF CONTENTS

"Overall, the body of research on pornography reveals a number of negative attitudes and behaviors that are connected with its use. It functions as a teacher, a permission-giver, and a trigger of these negative behaviors and attitudes. The damage is seen in men, women, and children, and to both married and single adults. It involves pathological behaviors, illegal behaviors, and some behaviors that are both illegal and pathological."

MARY ANNE LAYDEN

Director of the Sexual Trauma and Psychopathology Program
Center for Cognitive Therapy
Department of Psychiatry
University of Pennsylvania[1]

INTRODUCTION

The following monograph, *The Social Costs of Pornography: A Statement of Findings and Recommendations*, is the fruit of an inquiry begun at a consultation held in Princeton, New Jersey, in December 2008, sponsored by the Witherspoon Institute and cosponsored by the Institute for the Psychological Sciences.[2]

This consultation, which sought to estimate the social costs of pornography, was the first multifaceted, multidisciplinary, scholarly exploration in the internet age of a subject that is critically important to the health and well-being of many Americans: the hidden but real social toll of the current consumption of pornography—especially internet pornography—on an unprecedented scale.

---

[1] For a comprehensive review of the psychological research, see M. A. Layden, "Pornography and Violence: A New Look at the Research," in *The Social Costs of Pornography: A Collection of Papers*, eds. J. R. Stoner, Jr., and D. M. Hughes (Princeton, N.J.: Witherspoon Institute, 2010).

[2] The Witherspoon Institute is an independent research center located in Princeton, New Jersey; for more information, go to www.winst.org.

It is commonly observed that the history of pornography extends as far back in time as human civilization itself. Vase imagery from ancient Greece and the painted pornographic scenes at the ancient resort Pompeii are two frequently cited examples, though there are of course many more. The very concepts of "obscenity" and "pornography" have ancient Latin and Greek etymological roots.[3] No less ancient are prohibitions against pornographic images. These prohibitions have included the consistent condemnation of such material not only in Jewish, Christian, and Muslim moral thought, but also in secular law.[4] Pornography and obscenity have also been traditional objects of preoccupation for legislators and law enforcers in the United States and elsewhere. Two recent, prominent examples of such attempts to grapple with the multifaceted issues of pornography consumption are the 1986 Attorney General's Commission on Pornography, also known as the Meese Report, and the 1987 Report of the Surgeon General's Workshop on Pornography and Public Health.[5]

Nevertheless, despite the concern that pornography has traditionally raised both inside and outside the government, it is clear based on a variety of measures that today's internet pornography is qualitatively and quantitatively different from any that has come before. This is so for at least three reasons: (1) the ubiquity and accessibility of internet pornography; (2) the qualitative difference in imagery and "hard-core" nature of much of internet pornography; and (3) the sharply increased consumption of internet pornography.

Society has only begun to grapple with these new problems. This statement's purpose is to bring to public attention a voluminous amount of data now

---

[3] For a discussion of the origin of these words, see, for example, W. Kendrick, *The Secret Museum: Pornography in Modern Culture* (Berkeley: University of California Press, 1987), chap. 1, cited in J. R. Stoner, Jr., "Freedom, Virtue, and the Politics of Regulating Pornography," in *The Social Costs of Pornography: A Collection of Papers* (Princeton, N.J.: Witherspoon Institute, 2010).

[4] Stoner (2010). For a discussion of pornography and Islam, see H. Yusuf, "Desire and the Tainted Soul: Islamic Insights into Lust, Chastity, and Love," in *The Social Costs of Pornography: A Collection of Papers* (Princeton, N.J.: Witherspoon Institute, 2010).

[5] The abstract for the Surgeon General Report reads: "A panel of clinicians and researchers concluded that pornography does stimulate attitudes and behavior that lead to gravely negative consequences for individuals and for society and that these outcomes impair the mental, emotional, and physical health of children and adults." (PsycINFO Database Record (c) 2008 APA, all rights reserved.)

accumulating about contemporary pornography and its connections to a range of individual and social ills. The following findings explore these phenomena and their consequences in greater detail, drawing on the most compelling sources on this topic now available from a range of clinical and other professional disciplines.[6] The discussion that follows condenses a large amount of information, much of which could only be referenced in footnotes. Those interested in further reading are urged to consult the work cited in the footnotes of this text, including the papers from the Princeton consultation collected in *The Social Costs of Pornography: A Collection of Papers*, edited by James R. Stoner, Jr., and Donna M. Hughes.

PRELIMINARY COMMENTS

In order that the full import of that information be grasped, four points must be noted at the outset.

First, this statement represents a professional and expert agreement about the social ramifications of internet pornography that is relatively new, and which differs significantly from public understanding of the issue. This document intends to update public understanding by sharing information from a variety of sources that testify compellingly to the links between pornography consumption and a wide number of psychological, social, and family pathologies.

Second, some implications of the empirical evidence that follows are likely to cause controversy. This is so in part because the received opinion on pornography in our day tends to follow a libertarian sensibility, according to which the consumption of pornographic imagery amounts to victimless personal entertainment, however morally offensive it may be to some.

As understandable as that sensibility may be, it is falsified by a growing, multidimensional, empirical record of pornography's harms. As one clinician has testified, "Those who claim pornography is harmless entertainment, benign sexual expression, or a marital aid, have clearly never sat in a therapist's office with individuals, couples, or families who are reeling from the devastating

---

6   P. F. Fagan, "The Effects of Pornography on Individuals, Marriage, Family and Community," Family Research Council, 2009. See also Layden (2010).

9

effects of this material."[7] Research and data suggest that the habitual use of pornography—and especially of internet pornography—can have a range of damaging effects on human beings of all ages and of both sexes, affecting their happiness, their productivity, their relationships with one another, and their functioning in society. Drawing on data obtained by a variety of economic, clinical, and other tools, the pages ahead detail the manifold human costs of pornography.

Third, despite the expert agreement on these findings, much research remains to be done. Although the empirical record to date clearly suggests that pornography—especially of the hard-core and violent sort—is harmful, it is limited by several constraints. For one, internet pornography in particular is so new that more time will be required for a more in-depth study of the phenomenon. Further, the pornography industry is by nature diffuse and somewhat secretive, making reliable data hard to come by. In addition, consumers respond to surveys about their use of pornography less willingly than about other, more publicly discussed subjects. Nonetheless, much is already known—certainly enough to recommend guidelines for public action along the lines described at the end of this statement.

Finally, the concurrence of the signatories gathered here is all the more significant because of their diversity. Every major shade of religious belief is represented, from atheism and agnosticism to Christianity, Judaism, and Islam. Both the left and the right in American politics are represented, including social conservatism and contemporary feminism. A unique range of professional specialties also is represented, among them economics, medicine, psychiatry, psychology, philosophy, sociology, journalism, and law. Such broad agreement is rare on any subject. That it exists on the subject of contemporary pornography and its social costs is eloquent testimony to what is now known about the problems posed by what has been thought of (and is still frequently thought of) as a harmless and victimless pursuit.

---

[7]   J. C. Manning, "The Impact of Pornography on Women: Social Science Findings and Clinical Observations," in *The Social Costs of Pornography: A Collection of Papers* (Princeton, N.J.: Witherspoon Institute, 2010).

Numerous times while recounting their investigations of these issues, scholars have likened their efforts to those undertaken by health officials and other professionals concerned about tobacco use in the years before the Surgeon General's milestone 1964 report on that issue. Then as now, health professionals with the aid of scholars and other authorities took the lead in starting what turned out to be a dramatic, long-term turnaround in the consensus about a substance regarded by many Americans as harmless. Then as now, the activity in question was widely regarded as harmless—or at least as a practice that hurt no one other than the user. Decades later, thanks in part to their pioneering efforts at communicating an unpopular if true message about tobacco's harms, smoking has been largely stigmatized and curtailed. Few would argue that society is worse off for that dramatic change in personal behavior.

We believe that society will be similarly better off if the accumulating facts about the current use of pornography and its consequences are widely and effectively circulated so that people from all walks of life can take account of them.

The Witherspoon Institute
Princeton, New Jersey
February 2010

FINDING ONE

≋

Unlike at any other time in history, pornography is now available and consumed widely in our society, due in large part to the internet. No one remains untouched by it.

As mentioned in the Introduction, although pornography has existed for millennia, never has it been as widely available or used as it has been in recent years. Though researchers are only beginning to assemble reliable statistics regarding the increase in the consumption of pornography, lay and professional observers have already noted the obvious contribution of internet pornography to that dramatic rise.

Pamela Paul, a *TIME Magazine* reporter whose 2005 book *Pornified* is among the first general-interest, book-length examinations of this subject, said:

> Today, the number of people looking at pornography is staggering. Americans rent upwards of 800 million pornographic videos and DVDs (about one in five of all rented movies is porn), and the 11,000 porn films shot each year far outpaces Hollywood's yearly slate of 400. Four billion dollars a year is spent on video pornography in the United States, more than on football, baseball, and basketball. One in four internet users look at a pornography website in any given month. Men look at pornography online more than they look at any other subject. And 66% of 18–34-year-old men visit a pornographic site every month.[8]

Paul's observations are echoed in a recent issue of *The Atlantic* by writer Ross Douthat, whose essay "Is Pornography Adultery?" draws attention to the fact that the reach of contemporary pornography is something genuinely new:

---

[8]   P. Paul, "From Pornography to Porno to Porn: How Porn Became the Norm," in *The Social Costs of Pornography: A Collection of Papers* (Princeton, N.J.: Witherspoon Institute, 2010).

Over the past three decades, the VCR, on-demand cable service, and the internet have completely overhauled the ways in which people interact with porn.... Nothing in the long history of erotica compares with the way millions of Americans experience porn today, and our moral intuitions are struggling to catch up.[9]

Numerous statistics drawn from the 2008 Internet Pornography Statistics confirm the impression that pornography is widely accessed by internet users, and that both production and consumption are expanding. Every second, there are approximately 28,258 internet users viewing pornography. Every day, there are approximately 116,000 online searches for child pornography.[10] In 2005, 13,585 hard-core pornographic video/DVD titles were released in the United States, up from 1,300 titles in 1988. One recent study of undergraduate and graduate students ages eighteen to twenty-six around the country found that 69% of men and 10% of women in this sample viewed pornography more than once a month.[11]

Nor is there room for doubt that this consumption has parallels in the popular culture more broadly. The number of sex scenes in US television, for example, reportedly nearly doubled between 1998 and 2005.[12] Mainstream video games frequently feature pornographic themes; one called "Leisure Suit Larry," for example, features full-on nudity. The game's manufacturers fought to obtain an "M" rating (the equivalent of a film's "R") in order to ensure carriage at Wal-Mart Stores across the country.[13]

Many more examples could be offered, but the point remains: pornography is ubiquitous not only on the internet, but also in many other areas of popular

---

9   R. Douthat, "Is Pornography Adultery?" *The Atlantic*, October 2008.

10   J. Ropelato, "Internet Pornography Statistics," Internet Filter Learning Center, available at http://internet-filter-review.toptenreviews.com/internet-pornography-statistics.html.

11   J. S. Carroll, L. M. Padilla-Walker, L. J. Nelson, C. D. Olson, C. M. Barry, and S. D. Madsen, "Generation XXX: Pornography Acceptance and Use Among Emerging Adults," *Journal of Adolescent Research* 23, no. 1 (2008): 6–30.

12   D. Kunkel, K. Eyal, K. Finnerty, E. Biely, and E. Donnerstein, *Sex on TV 4* (Menlo Park, Calif.: Kaiser Family Foundation, 2005).

13   C. Morris, "Video Games Get Raunchy," CNNMoney.com, May 13, 2004.

entertainment, including juvenile entertainment. Particularly troubling are the consequences of this ubiquity for children and adolescents. By numerous measures, they are being exposed via the internet in unprecedented numbers to pornographic material—often involuntarily.

This new ubiquity of pornographic representation has altered our notion of what constitutes harm to individuals. As one clinician has noted:

> Prior to the advent of the internet, the pornography debate was entrenched in linear, cause-and-effect assumptions: a focus on the individual as the consumer or victim; legal, feminist, or moral perspectives; and disputes over the often-delicate continuum between censorship and freedom of speech. In today's internet-era, however, the debate and its core assumptions desperately need revising, if not a major overhaul, in order to address the fact that people of all ages, genders, and socio-economic groups are being exposed to and impacted by pornography.[14]

In sum, there is evidence that more people—children, adolescents, and adults—are consuming pornography—sporadically, inadvertently, or chronically—than ever before. The following sections of the statement bring newly available empirical evidence to bear on the consequences of that consumption for men, women, children, and society at large.

---

[14]   J. C. Manning, "The Impact of Pornography Upon Women," unpublished paper presented at a consultation on "The Social Costs of Pornography," at Princeton University, December 12, 2008; on file at the Witherspoon Institute.

FINDING TWO

≋

There is abundant empirical evidence that this pornography is qualitatively different from any that has gone before, in several ways: its ubiquity, the use of increasingly realistic streaming images, and the increasingly "hard-core" character of what is consumed.

Internet pornography is historically unique not only because of its ubiquity but also because of its nature, especially in two respects: (1) its potential addictiveness and (2) its (increasing) realism.

Not all consumers of internet pornography are chronic users, nor are all unable to resist pursuing it to the detriment of other activities. As with tobacco, part of the difficulty in measuring the "harm" of internet pornography is that it does not affect all individuals in the same way. In some cases a casual, sporadic user may be harmed by his pornography habit more than a chronic, daily user. We might also discover that some people are more predisposed toward heavy pornography consumption than are others. These and other areas of research remain to be explored.

Nonetheless, internet pornography does evoke in some users those behaviors that clinical and psychological literature calls "addiction," just as in cases of addiction to alcohol, nicotine, and other substances.[15] The addiction to pornography can even become "compulsive," meaning that it continues despite negative consequences to a person's functioning in his or her work

---

15 See, for example, P. Carnes, *Out of the Shadows: Understanding Sexual Addiction* (Center City, Minn.: Hazelden, 1992); A. Cooper, D. L. Delmonico, and R. Burg, "Cybersex Users, Abusers, and Compulsives: New Findings and Implications," *Sexual Addiction & Compulsivity: The Journal of Treatment and Prevention* 7, nos. 1–2 (2000): 5–29.

or relationships.[16] As one researcher has noted, "The negative effects of compulsive use—use that occurred despite negative consequences to the person's occupational or relationship functioning—may be obvious, such as the loss of a job due to surfing adult websites on the company computer, but may be more insidious, such as role disruption that occurs when a husband spends significant portions of his evenings online masturbating to explicit images rather than being with his family."[17]

Although not all of the complexities of the addiction model apply to pornography, the clinical and empirical record shows that to call the chronic consumption of pornography "dependency" or "addiction" is appropriate. To give one example of the addictive behaviors related to pornography, "what is considered normal (that is, what the average person does) is skewed for heavy users of pornography in such a way that they are unable to recognize just how uncommon their own behavior may be." Such normalization leads to an "over-estimation of how frequently certain sexual activities are actually practiced," which in turn increases one's willingness to do formerly unconscionable things, as demonstrated in research on adolescent boys.[18] Such behavior was rarely associated with pornography until the internet made the instantaneous acquisition of pornographic images possible at any time.

THE PECULIAR NATURE OF INTERNET PORNOGRAPHY MAKES ADDICTION MORE LIKELY.

As Douthat noted in *The Atlantic*, "Innovation has piled on innovation, making modern pornography a more immediate, visceral, and personalized experience."

---

[16]   See, for example, A. Cooper, C. R. Scherer, S. C. Boies, and B. L. Gordon, "Sexuality on the Internet: From Sexual Exploration to Pathological Expression," *Professional Psychology: Research and Practice* 30 (1999): 154–64; and M. P. Kafka, "The Paraphilia-Related Disorders: Nonparaphilic Hypersexuality and Sexual Compulsivity/Addiction," in *Principles and Practice of Sex Therapy*, 3rd ed., eds. S. R. Leiblum and R. C. Rosen (New York: Guilford Press, 2000): 471–503.

[17]   A. J. Bridges, "Pornography's Effects on Interpersonal Relationships," in *The Social Costs of Pornography: A Collection of Papers* (Princeton, N.J.: Witherspoon Institute, 2010).

[18]   Ibid.

This increasingly visceral experience has lately been further explained by contemporary advances in neuroscience. One scientist describes it as follows:[19]

> Pornography is more exciting than satisfying because we have two separate pleasure systems in our brains, one that has to do with exciting pleasure and one with satisfying pleasure. The exciting system relates to the 'appetitive' pleasure that we get imaging something we desire, such as sex or a good meal. Its neurochemistry is largely dopamine-related, and it raises our tension level.
>
> The second pleasure system has to do with the satisfaction, or consummatory pleasure, that attends actually having sex or having that meal, a calming, fulfilling pleasure. Its neurochemistry is based on the release of endorphins, which are related to opiates and give a peaceful, euphoric bliss.
>
> Pornography, by offering an endless harem of sexual objects, hyper-activates the appetitive system. Porn viewers develop new maps in their brains, based on the photos and videos they see. Because it is a use-it-or-lose-it brain, when we develop a map area, we long to keep it activated. Just as our muscles become impatient for exercise if we've been sitting all day, so too our senses hunger to be stimulated. The men at their computers [addicted to] looking at porn [are] uncannily like the rats in the cages of the NIH, pressing the bar to get a shot of dopamine or its equivalent. Though they [don't] know it, they [have] been seduced into pornographic training sessions that [meet] all the conditions required for plastic change of brain maps.[19]

This neurological change is reflected in reports of those who develop pornography addiction or dependence. Based on interviews with over

---

[19]   N. Doidge, *The Brain That Changes Itself: Stories of Personal Triumph from the Frontiers of Brain Science* (New York: Viking, 2007), p. 108.

one hundred heterosexual consumers of internet pornography (80% of them male), Pamela Paul observes:

> . . . lest pornography get written off as a "women's problem," consider the extensive effects of pornography on the primary users, men . . . . Countless men have described to me how, while using pornography, they have lost the ability to relate to or be close to women. They have trouble being turned on by "real" women, and their sex lives with their girlfriends or wives collapse. These are men who seem like regular guys, but who spend hours each week with porn—usually online. And many of them admit they have trouble cutting down their use. They also find themselves seeking out harder and harder pornography.[20]

The combination of hyper-realistic imagery, moving pictures, and rapid-fire bombardment of images appears to mean also that chronic consumers both become visually desensitized, and find themselves viewing depictions they themselves would once have regarded as taboo or off-limits.

This de-sensitization brought on by the barrage of imagery is familiar among therapists. One phenomenon described numerous times at the consultation was the way in which images that would initially disgust the viewer—including unwanted pop-ups such as child pornography or violent pornographic images encountered during the search for non-violent images—lose their ability to shock and disgust over time.

British writer Sean Thomas, in a widely read article published in the London *Spectator* in 2003 about his own pornography addiction, provided a vivid account of his personal descent into consumption of imagery that would once have revolted him:

> My interest in spanking got me speculating: what other kinks was I harboring? What other secret and rewarding corners lurked in my sexuality that I would now be able to investigate

---

[20]   Paul (2010).

in the privacy of my home? Plenty as it turned out. I discovered a serious penchant for inter alia, lesbian gynecology, interracial hard-core, and images of Japanese girls taking off their hot pants. I was also into netball players with no knickers, drunk Russian girls exposing themselves, and convoluted scenarios where submissive Danish actresses were intimately shaved by their dominant female partners in the shower. The Net had, in other words, revealed to me that I had an unquantifiable variety of sexual fantasies and quirks and that the process of satisfying these desires online only led to more interest.[21]

Most notably, and most alarmingly, numerous users have described both to reporters and to clinicians the apparent slippery slope from using pornography featuring adults to using child pornography.

PORNOGRAPHY IS INCREASINGLY HARD-CORE.

Therapists and others agree that pornography is not only more common now, but also increasingly "edgy." One observer notes:

> Even those who make no use of these "services" experience the cultural effects of saturation, as ordinary television, respectable magazines, and popular songs regularly include provocative images, situations, and lyrics that a generation ago would have been labeled "soft porn." Reports from those who have looked describe what now counts as "hard-core" in terms that would astonish the imagination and shock the conscience of anyone who is not a hard-core pornography user himself.[22]

In sum, today's pornography is both qualitatively and quantitatively different from any that has come before—and that qualitative difference includes for at least some consumers a slippery slope into ever more hard-core, sexually fetishistic, and formerly shocking imagery.

---

21   S. Thomas, "Self-Abuse," *Spectator* (London), June 28, 2003.

22   J. R. Stoner, Jr., "Taking a New Look at Pornography," *Public Discourse: Ethics, Law, and the Common Good*, February 9, 2009; available at http://www.thepublicdiscourse.com/2009/02/89.

FINDING THREE

≋

Today's consumption of internet pornography
can harm women in particular.

Internet pornography can cause particular harm to women, be they girlfriends or wives of consumers, or consumers themselves. Indeed any woman can be affected, insofar as pornography shapes cultural expectations about female sexual behavior (see finding five for more on how pornography shapes expectations about female sexual behavior).

By a variety of measures, internet pornography poses particular issues of health and well-being among wives whose husbands are consumers, and among other women involved in a serious, ostensibly monogamous relationship with a consumer.

In North American and Western European culture, wives generally seek marital relationships founded upon mutual respect, honesty, shared power, and romantic love. Pornography as depicted on the internet enshrines the opposite: relationships based on disrespect, detachment, promiscuity, and often abuse. This difference gives rise to unique distress and harm when a wife finds that her husband has been secretly using internet pornography.

Several researchers report that women typically feel betrayal, loss, mistrust, devastation, and anger as a result of the discovery of a partner's pornography use and/or online sexual activity.[23] In addition to the psychic costs of such discovery, there are other harms, among them a markedly increased likelihood

---

[23]   See, for example, A. J. Bridges, R. M. Bergner, and M. Hesson-McInniss, "Romantic Partners' Use of Pornography: Its Significance for Women," *Journal of Sex and Marital Therapy* 29, no. 1 (January/February 2003): 1–14; J. C. Manning, "A Qualitative Study of the Supports Women Find Most Beneficial When Dealing with a Spouse's Sexually Addictive or Compulsive Sexual Behavior," unpublished doctoral dissertation, Brigham Young University, Utah, 2006; and J. P. Schneider, "Effects of Cybersex Addiction on the Family: Results of a Survey," *Sexual Addiction & Compulsivity* 7, nos. 1–2 (2000): 31–58.

of divorce and family break-up. At the November 2003 meeting of the American Academy of Matrimonial Lawyers (comprising the nation's top 1,600 divorce and matrimonial law attorneys), 62% of the 350 attendees said the internet had played a role in divorces they had handled during the last year, and 56% of the divorce cases involved one party having an obsessive interest in pornographic websites.[24]

Finally, wives and other sexual partners of pornography consumers have heightened health risks as a result of the increased likelihood of the consumer's exposure to other partners. One nationally representative study of 531 internet users published in 2004 found that those who had had an extramarital affair were more than three times more likely to have used internet pornography than were internet users who had not had an affair. According to the same study, people who had engaged in paid sex or prostitution were almost four times more likely to have used internet pornography than those who had not engaged in paid sex.[25] Other studies, including experimental research that compares men exposed to pornography in laboratory settings with a control group of men exposed to innocuous situation comedies, also indicate that the consumption of pornography leads men to place less value on sexual fidelity and more value on casual sex; on average, men who are exposed to pornography in a lab setting also become more aggressive compared to men who are exposed to non-sexual material, and this is particularly true for the men who are exposed to the most hard-core sexual imagery.[26]

In a currently ongoing study into the effects of pornography on adult relationships, economists Kirk Doran and Joseph Price are examining data from the General Social Survey (GSS) to assess the impact of pornography use on measures of marital well-being, including on divorce, extramarital sex, reported happiness of the marriage, and overall reported happiness.[27] They report that among individuals who have ever been married, those who report

---

[24] Cited in P. Paul, "The Porn Factor," *TIME Magazine* (January 19, 2004).

[25] S. Stack, I. Wasserman, and R. Kern, "Adult Social Bonds and Use of Internet Pornography," *Social Science Quarterly* 85, no. 1 (March 2004): 75–88.

[26] Carroll et al. (2008); D. Zillmann and J. Bryant, "Pornography's Impact on Sexual Satisfaction," *Journal of Applied Social Psychology* 18, no. 5 (1988): 438–53.

[27] K. Doran and J. Price, "Movies and Marriage: Do Some Films Harm Marital Happiness?," in progress, 2009.

having seen an X-rated movie in the last year are 25.6% more likely to be divorced, 65.1% more likely to report having had an extramarital affair, 8.0% less likely to report having a "very happy" marriage (if they are still married), and 13.1% less likely to report being "very happy" with life in general. Even though the initial research does not allow us to make definitive social scientific claims about the effects of pornography, it clearly indicates that pornography consumption is linked to a higher risk of adverse outcomes in various areas.

To quote a scholar at the consultation, "internet pornography is often associated with activities that undermine marital exclusivity and fidelity and increase the risk of contracting and transmitting sexual diseases."[28]

Though by a wide variety of measures most consumers of internet pornography are male, there is nevertheless evidence that women are increasing their consumption as well. One study suggests that women now represent as much as 30% of internet pornography consumers.[29] Similarly, a 2008 study of college-age students found that 31% of young women reported using pornography (versus 87% for men) in the last year.[30]

---

[28]   Manning (2006).
[29]   Internet Pornography Statistics, 2008; Nielsen/NetRatings, April 2005.
[30]   Carroll et al. (2008).

FINDING FOUR

≋

*Today's consumption of internet pornography
can harm children in particular.*

The few statistics available about the use of pornography by children and adolescents are even more difficult to assess than those concerning adults. Few parents would allow their children to be research subjects in such an area, and researchers do not have reliable access to children and adolescents without their parents' consent.

Nevertheless, there can be no doubt that children and adolescents are far more exposed to pornography via the internet than they ever have been before. One 2004 study by Columbia University, for example, found that 11.5 million teenagers (45%) have friends who regularly view internet pornography and download it.[31] The prevalence of teens with friends who view internet pornography increases with age. Boys are significantly more likely than girls to have friends who view online pornography. In one study, 65% of boys ages 16 and 17 reported that they had friends who regularly viewed and downloaded internet pornography.[32]

Despite the illegality of marketing sexually explicit material to minors, the pornography industry does not effectively deny access to young consumers. Approximately 75% of pornographic websites display visual teasers on the homepages before asking if the viewers are of legal age; only 3% of such websites require proof-of-age before granting access to sexually explicit material, and two-thirds of pornographic websites do not include any adult-

---

[31]   National Survey of American Attitudes on Substance Abuse IX: Teen Dating Practices and Sexual Activity, The National Center on Addiction and Substance Abuse at Columbia University, p. 6; cited in C. C. Radsch, "Teenagers' Sexual Activity Is Tied to Drugs and Drink," *New York Times*, August 20, 2004, p. A14.
[32]   National Survey of American Attitudes on Substance Abuse IX: Teen Dating Practices and Sexual Activity, The National Center on Addiction and Substance Abuse at Columbia University, p. 23.

content warnings.[33] Nor are there effective filtering systems widely in place on cell phones with internet access or iPods that can transmit "podnography," despite the popularity of such contemporary media among adolescents.[34]

Some of this contact is unsought. In one study funded by the US Congress through the National Center for Missing and Exploited Children, the authors concluded that sexually explicit material on the internet is "very intrusive" and can be inadvertently stumbled upon while searching for other material or when opening e-mail.[35] In a more recent study by the same authors, 34% of adolescents reported being exposed to unwanted sexual content online, a figure that appears to have risen by 9% over the last five years. This 2006 Youth Internet Safety Survey of 1,500 representative youth found that one in seven reported unwanted sexual solicitation, and one in eleven had been harassed online.[36] A 2002 Henry J. Kaiser Family Foundation Report found that 70% of youth ages fifteen to seventeen reported accidentally coming across pornography online, and 23% of those youth said that this happened "very" or "somewhat" often.[37]

Furthermore, such numbers do not even take into account how often young people are exposed to pornographic materials via media other than the internet. Pornography and pornographic references are frequently laced into popular video games, advertisements, television, and music, and also

---

[33]   D. Thornburgh and H. S. Lin, eds., *Youth, Pornography, and the Internet* (Washington, D.C.: National Academy Press, 2002), pp. 78-79.

[34]   D. L. Delmonico and E. J. Griffin, "Cybersex and the E-Teen: What Marriage and Family Therapists Should Know," *Journal of Marital & Family Therapy* 34, no. 4 (October 2008): 431–44.

[35]   K. J. Mitchell, D. Finkelhor, and J. Wolak, "The Exposure of Youth to Unwanted Sexual Material on the Internet: A National Survey of Risk, Impact, and Prevention," *Youth & Society* 34, no. 3 (2003): 330–58; K. J. Mitchell, D. Finkelhor, and J. Wolak, "Victimization of Youths on the Internet," in *The Victimization of Children: Emerging Issues* (Binghamton, N.Y.: Haworth Maltreatment & Trauma Press, 2003).

[36]   J. Wolak, K. J. Mitchell, D. Finkelhor, "Online Victimization of Youth: Five Years Later," 2006: 7, 10, available at http://www.unh.edu/ccrc/pdf/CV138.pdf.

[37]   The Henry J. Kaiser Family Foundation Report, 2002.

are ubiquitous in music videos.[38] There is also the growing phenomenon of "sexting," or sending pornographic images via text messaging, which is raising unprecedented legal and other issues across the country. The combined effect of these proliferating images and references is that many more young people experience pornography through a variety of media, with consequences that are similarly varied.

The foregoing research corroborates the fears and experience of caretakers of children everywhere: pornography has infected modern childhood. Some parents worry about what their sons are doing while they use the internet for schoolwork. Others wonder what the male peers of their daughters are viewing online. Some adults directly witness the infiltration of pornography into the lives of the children for whom they care, catching them acting out pornographic films or viewing pornography at local libraries. In the news one often finds stories of "child pornography arrests, and school incidents in which teachers are caught looking at pornography on school computers during school hours."[39]

Child psychologists report similar experiences and concerns. "Kids today are going to run into pornography online, not erotica," as one Massachusetts psychologist puts it. "They're getting a very bad model. Pornography doesn't show how a real couple negotiates conflict or creates intimacy." She further worries that internet pornography, much of which is "rape-like," is "a brutal way to be introduced to sexuality." The clinical director of Masters and Johnson reports seeing fourteen- and fifteen-year-old boys who are addicted to pornography: "It's awful to see the effect it has on them; at such a young age, to have that kind of sexual problem." A psychologist who runs the Coche Center in Philadelphia describes one case in which an eleven-year-old girl was found creating her own pornographic website, explaining that pornography is considered "cool" among her friends. The Coche psychologist

---

[38]   See, for example, D. Levin and J. Kilbourne, *So Sexy So Soon: The New Sexualized Childhood and What Parents Can Do to Protect Their Kids* (New York: Ballantine Books, 2008), pp. 142–47; M. Moore, "Rapelay Virtual Rape Game Banned By Amazon," *Telegraph*, February 13, 2009, available at http://www.telegraph.co.uk/scienceandtechnology/technology/4611161/Rapelay-virtual-rape-game-banned-by-Amazon.html; M. Edlund, "MUSIC; Hip-Hop's Crossover to The Adult Aisle," *New York Times*, March 7, 2004.
[39]   Paul (2010).

also says that more boys, including pre-adolescents, are being treated for pornography addiction, adding, "Before the internet, I never encountered this."[40]

Pamela Paul, a participant in the Princeton consultation, expressed a reaction to these facts that many people share:

> It is terrible enough that adults are suffering the consequences of a pornified culture. But we must think about the kind of world we are introducing to our children. Certainly everyone—liberals and conservatives alike—can agree with the statement, "It wasn't like this when we were kids." And I can't imagine anyone would have that thought without simultaneously experiencing a profound sense of fear and loss.[41]

But is there evidence that this exposure is harmful to children?

For some people, no more evidence is needed. However, even skeptics could not deny the evidence of harmfulness that is emerging in clinical settings. For one thing, some children and adolescents feel so harmed that they are presenting themselves for treatment. Further, a study of 804 representative Italian teenagers found that boys who viewed pornography were significantly more likely to report having "sexually harassed a peer or having forced somebody to have sex."[42]

Another study of 101 sexually abusive children in Australia documented increased aggressiveness in boys who used pornography. A quarter of the participants said that an older sibling or a friend had shown them how to access this material; another quarter said that using pornography was their primary reason for going online. This study points to one more troubling fact about the access of children today to the internet, including internet

---

[40] Ibid.

[41] Ibid.

[42] S. Bonino, S. Ciairano, E. Rabaglietti, and E. Cattelino, "Use of Pornography and Self-Reported Engagement in Sexual Violence Among Adolescents," *European Journal of Developmental Psychology* 3 (2006): 265–88.

pornography: their parents are almost all unaware of what they are doing. Nearly all of those parents independently reported that they doubted that their child would access pornography on the internet.[43]

In addition, there is abundant evidence that children and adolescents use pornography to coerce each other into sexual behavior, while adults also groom or coerce children by the same means. One therapist reports, "I am also witnessing more female adolescents tolerating emotional, physical, and sexual abuse in dating relationships, feeling pressure to make out with females as a way to turn guys on, looking at or producing pornography so that their boyfriends will think they are 'open-minded' and 'cool,' and normalizing sexual abuse done to them because they see the same acts eroticized in pornography."[44] Indeed, one recent study finds that adolescent girls who report using pornography are more likely to report being victims of passive violence, where they experience sexual harassment or forced sex at the hands of male friends or acquaintances.[45]

A study focusing on juvenile sex offenders found that a disproportionate number of such offenders had been exposed to pornography as a child; specifically, twenty-nine of the thirty juvenile sex offenders had been exposed to X-rated magazines or videos, and the average age of first exposure was about seven-and-one-half years.[46]

The signatories contend that even the most extreme libertarians who argue that children should be allowed to view such materials must take these various harms into account. After all, defenders of the circulation of pornography among adults justify themselves primarily on the claim that adult consumers know the difference between reality (sex with real people) and cyber-reality (contrived scenes of rape and violence). However, neither children, nor perhaps even adolescents, can easily make that distinction.

---

[43]   P. Goodenough, "Online Porn Driving Sexually Aggressive Children," CNSNews.com, November 26, 2003.

[44]   Manning (2006).

[45]   Bonino et al. (2006).

[46]   E. Wieckowski, P. Hartsoe, A. Mayer, and J. Shortz, "Deviant Sexual Behavior in Children and Young Adolescents: Frequency and Patterns," *Sexual Abuse: A Journal of Research and Treatment* 10, no. 4 (1998): 293–304.

In sum, there is evidence that the prevalence of pornography in the lives of many children and adolescents is far more significant than most adults realize, that pornography is deforming the healthy sexual development of these young viewers, and that it is used to exploit children and adolescents.

FINDING FIVE

≋

Today's consumption of internet pornography can harm people not immediately connected to consumers of pornography.

Though most of the testimony provided at the Princeton consultation concerned those immediately affected by today's levels of pornography consumption, other people whose lives are influenced by such consumption should also be considered in the assessment of pornography's wider social impact.

HARM TO VICTIMS OF SEXUAL EXPLOITATION

Although empirical evidence abounds on the toll that internet pornography can exact from consumers and their families, much less is known about the toll on those who create these materials. However, preliminary evidence is compelling enough to confirm that those on the "supply" side of the business, those who create the sexual imagery in the first place, are also harmed by pornography.

Some of this harm is distributed among the most vulnerable. Women of all ages comprise 80% of those trafficked, children comprise 50%, and of those women and children 70% are used for sexual exploitation. The federal government estimates that 14,500 to 17,500 people are trafficked into the United States each year. "The Department of Justice and the National Center for Missing and Exploited Children both recognize that pornography is an element that adds to the serious problem of sex trafficking. Many traffickers are found with filming equipment and cameras to create and sell pornography."[47]

Other sources suggest that the lives of performers in the "sex industry" are far from enviable, and are instead often beset with exploitation, drug use, disease, and other afflictions. A recent memoir by a woman who was formerly

---

[47] E. McGinnis, *The Horrifying Reality of Sex Trafficking*, available at beverlylahayeinstitute.org.

employed as a Playboy "Bunny" reviews related problems in detail and with frequent references to drugs, exploitation, and unsafe sexual practices.[48]

Moreover, pornography has been implicated in some sexual assaults, though the precise causal relationship between sexual assault and pornography use remains controversial among many academics. One study conducting interviews with 200 prostitutes found that about a quarter of them mentioned pornography being intimately tied to a sexual assault they had experienced, with the abuser making reference to something he had seen as inspiration for his acting or insisting that the woman enjoyed the assault.[49] Moreover, a number of studies using representative samples of men have found a link between pornography consumption and higher levels of sexual aggression on the part of men.[50]

Obviously, many people view pornography, including violent pornography, without acting out what they have seen. But as long as some pornography consumers are inspired by such scenes to imitate violent acts or to act against minors, pornography will be implicated in such criminal behavior.

HARM TO FEMALE ADOLESCENTS

Female adolescents are put uniquely at risk by pornography at today's scale.

One therapist who works routinely with young women noted that despite the greater opportunities available to her, a female born today will find herself "introduced into a society that is arguably more sexually coarse, explicit, confusing, and risky than that of previous eras." Because of "modern trends in pornography consumption and production, sexualized media, sex crime, sexually transmitted diseases, online sexual predators, internet dating services,

---

[48]   I. St. James, *Bunny Tales* (Philadelphia: Running Press Book Publishers, 2006).

[49]   M. H. Silbert and A. M. Pines, "Pornography and Sexual Abuse of Women," *Sex Roles* 10, nos. 11–12 (1984): 857–68.

[50]   See, for example, M. Allen, D. D'Alessio, and K. Brezgel, "A Meta-Analysis Summarizing the Effects of Pornography II: Aggression After Exposure," *Human Communication Research* 22, no. 2 (December 1995): 258–83; Bonino, Ciairano, Rabaglietti, Cattelino (2006); N. M. Malamuth, T. Addison, and M. Koss, "Pornography and Sexual Aggression: Are There Reliable Effects and Can We Understand Them?" *Annual Review of Sex Research* 11 (2000): 26–91.

and sexualized cyber bullying," the woman of today lives in a "world more sexually distorting, daunting, and aggressive than ever before, and at earlier ages in her development than ever before."[51]

Various findings from social science confirm the harm that the pornographic culture does to female adolescents.

First, several academic studies have suggested that both adolescent boys and girls who are exposed to a sexualized media environment are more likely to view women as sexual objects.[52] In one widely reported study in February 2009, Susan Fiske, professor of psychology at Princeton University, used MRI scans to analyze the brain activity of men viewing pornography. The results showed that, after viewing pornographic images, men looked at women more as objects than as humans. One conclusion drawn by Fiske was that, "When there are sexualized images in the workplace, it's hard for people not to think about their female colleagues in those terms."[53]

Second, pornography raises risks to the physical health of adolescent girls. Habituation to pornographic imagery predisposes some adolescent girls to engage in sexually risky behavior. Three separate studies found a strong association between pornography consumption and engaging in oral and anal sexual intercourse among adolescents.[54] This was so even though the

---

[51]   Manning (2010).

[52]   L. M. Ward, "Does Television Exposure Affect Emerging Adults' Attitudes and Assumptions About Sexual Relationships? Correlational and Experimental Confirmation," *Journal of Youth and Adolescence* 31, no. 1 (2002). See also L. M. Ward and K. Friedman, "Using TV as a Guide: Associations Between Television Viewing and Adolescents' Sexual Attitudes and Behavior," *Journal of Research on Adolescents* 16, no. 1 (March 2006): 133-56; and J. Peter and P. M. Valkenburg, "Adolescents' Exposure to a Sexualized Media Environment and Their Notions of Women as Sex Objects," *Sex Roles* 56 (February 2007): 381–95.

[53]   Quoted in I. Sample, *The Guardian* (UK), "Sex Objects: Pictures Shift Men's View of Women," February 16, 2009, available at http://www.guardian.co.uk/science/2009/feb/16/sex-object-photograph.

[54]   C. Rogala and T. Tydén, "Does Pornography Influence Young Women's Sexual Behavior?" *Women's Health Issues* 13, no. 1 (January 2003): 39–43; T. Tydén and C. Rogala, "Sexual Behavior Among Young Men in Sweden and the Impact of Pornography," *International Journal of STD & AIDS* 15, no. 9 (2004): 590–93; and E. Haggström-Nordin, U. Hanson, and T. Tydén, "Associations Between Pornography Consumption and Sexual Practices Among Adolescents in Sweden," *International Journal of STD & AIDS* 16, no. 2 (March 2005): 102–07.

35

majority of females described anal intercourse as a negative experience.[55] Such behavioral trends, combined with the fact that condom use has been found to be low among those engaging in anal sex (40% by one estimate), raise health issues for both sexes.[56] The risks are arguably more acute for heterosexual female adolescents than for heterosexual male adolescents, since females are more likely to be exposed to sexually transmitted diseases via anal and oral-genital contact.

Third, research with first-year college students suggests several troubling consequences of the exposure to sexually explicit material.[57] These include (but are not limited to) increased tolerance toward sexually explicit material, thereby requiring more novel or bizarre material to achieve the same level of arousal or interest; misperceptions about exaggerated sexual activity in the general populace and the prevalence of less common sexual practices such as group sex, bestiality, and sadomasochistic activity; increased risk of developing a negative body image, especially for women; and acceptance of promiscuity as a normal state of interaction. Also, as noted above, teenage girls who are exposed to pornography are also much more likely to be the victims of unwanted sexual violence.[58] Such outcomes are obviously negative for both sexes, but the normalization of promiscuity puts adolescent females at even higher risk for sexually transmitted disease.

HARM TO ALL OF SOCIETY RESULTING FROM THE BREAKDOWN OF FAMILIES

To the extent that the consumption of internet pornography is one more factor subverting family life, it harms not only those affected immediately by the user but also the wider society as well. An abundance of empirical research available elsewhere testifies to the relationship between family stability and desirable individual and social outcomes.[59]

---

55 Rogala and Tydén (2003).

56 Ibid.

57 D. Zillman, "Influence of Unrestrained Access to Erotica on Adolescents' and Young Adults' Dispositions Toward Sexuality," *Journal of Adolescent Health* 27 (2000): 41-44; Carroll et al. (2008).

58 Bonino et al. (2006).

59 See, for example, *Marriage and the Public Good: Ten Principles*, a statement detailing the benefits of marriage and signed by seventy scholars (Princeton, N.J.: Witherspoon Institute, 2008); Bridges (2010).

FINDING SIX

≋

The consumption of internet pornography can harm its consumers.

Typically, the chronic consumer of pornography is male. By most statistical measures as well as by anecdotal evidence, men are far more likely to pursue pornography, including internet pornography, than are women.

This does not mean that the damaging effects of chronic use among women do not exist. However, the sexual imbalance in consumption does mean that empirical evidence of the effects of internet pornography on men is more abundant and available than of the effects on women. There appear to be several adverse effects on some men who use internet pornography.

PORNOGRAPHY USE UNDERMINES MARITAL AND OTHER INTIMATE RELATIONSHIPS.

As already noted, the fallout from the consumption of internet pornography can be catastrophic for the woman who discovers that her husband or boyfriend has been using it in secret. The harm of this fallout obviously extends to the man himself.

Men who use pornography are also less attractive to potential female partners. In one recent study of college men and women, researchers found that, "For women, frequent pornography use in a potential mate resulted in significantly lower intentions to pursue him for a relationship."[60]

---

[60]   T. McGahan and A. J. Bridges, "What Traits Do Men and Women Want in a Romantic Partner? Stated Preferences Versus Actual Behavior," in progress.

Pornography use can make men sexually incompetent with a real partner.

Perhaps the most paradoxical fallout of the pursuit of sexual gratification via internet pornography is that it can render the chronic user incapable of the very sexual satisfaction that he is seeking. As one doctor specializing in neuropsychiatry related, a number of the men whom he treated in the mid- to late- 1990s had become so dependent upon pornographic images to become sexually aroused that they were no longer attracted enough to their wives to have intercourse with them.[61] Moreover, research suggests that exposure to pornography decreases sexual satisfaction with one's partner for both men *and* women.[62]

In addition, chronic pornography use is associated with depression and unhappiness. As the doctor quoted earlier summarizes, "Pornographers promise healthy pleasure and relief from sexual tension, but what they often deliver is an addiction, tolerance, and an eventual decrease in pleasure. Paradoxically, the male patients I worked with often craved pornography but didn't like it."[63] A professor of philosophy explains the relation between pornography use and unhappiness in broader terms:

> Sex, portrayed in the porno-image, is an affair of attractive people with every technical accomplishment. Most people are not attractive, and with only second-class equipment. Once they are led by their porn addiction to see sex in the instrumentalized way that pornography encourages, they begin to lose confidence in their ability to enjoy sex in any other way than through fantasy. People who lose confidence in their ability to attract soon become unattractive.

> And then the fear of desire arises, and from that fear the fear of love. This, it seems to me, is the real risk attached to

---

61 N. Doidge, *The Brain That Changes Itself: Stories of Personal Triumph from the Frontiers of Brain Science* (New York: Viking, 2007), p. 104.
62 Zillman and Bryant (1988).
63 Doidge (2007).

pornography. Those who become addicted to this risk-free form of sex run a risk of another and greater kind. They risk the loss of love, in a world where only love brings happiness.[64]

PORNOGRAPHY USE APPEARS TO BE FOR SOME A SLIPPERY SLOPE UPON WHICH THE CONSUMER FINDS HIMSELF ULTIMATELY DRAWN TO INCREASINGLY "EDGY" MATERIAL.

Numerous clinicians have testified that users report disgust and shame at finding themselves stimulated by images that once would have repulsed them. This process is known to therapists as "habituation." As journalist Pamela Paul summarized, based on her interviews with frequent consumers,

> Men ... told me that they found themselves wasting countless hours looking at pornography on their televisions and DVD players, and especially online. They looked at things they would have once considered appalling—bestiality, group sex, hard-core S&M, genital torture, child pornography.

> They found the way they looked at women in real life warping to fit the pornography fantasies they consumed onscreen. . . . They worried about the way they saw their daughters and girls their daughters' age. It wasn't only their sex lives that suffered—pornography's effects rippled out, touching all aspects of their existence. Their work days became interrupted, their hobbies were tossed aside, their family lives were disrupted. Some men even lost their jobs, their wives, and their children. The sacrifice is enormous.[65]

Pornography use also desensitizes some users to themes of violence.[66] This is all the more concerning given the ubiquity of violence in pornographic material. One 2007 analysis of fifty best-selling adult videos reported that

---

64   R. Scruton, "The Abuse of Sex," in *The Social Costs of Pornography: A Collection of Papers* (Princeton, N.J.: Witherspoon Institute, 2010).
65   Paul (2010).
66   Bridges (2010).

nearly half of the 304 scenes contained verbal aggression, and over 88% showed physical aggression.[67]

PORNOGRAPHY USE IS GENERATING A SERIES OF COTTAGE INDUSTRIES AS SOME USERS ATTEMPT TO CURTAIL OR CEASE THEIR CONSUMPTION. THESE INDUSTRIES PROVE THAT SOME USERS PERCEIVE THEMSELVES TO BE HARMED BY SUCH CONSUMPTION.

One interesting measure of the harm of pornography is the magnitude of efforts by some consumers to extricate themselves from addiction to internet pornography.

Like the lawyers in the example cited earlier who report that internet pornography is increasingly a feature of divorce cases, those involved in the help and counseling fields report that internet pornography is a rapidly growing component of their caseloads. A psychologist and former director of the Masters and Johnson Institute in St. Louis, Missouri, reports seeing such cases at an "epidemic" level.[68]

Entrepreneurs are also finding niches in the market for products aimed at helping consumers control personal pornography consumption. Books are being published designed to break the habit, and software developers are selling filters designed to prevent temptation, though the effectiveness of these filters is in doubt.[69]

In economic terms, spending for the sake of breaking the habit of pornography consumption has grown along with spending on the consumption of pornography. No one would seek such treatment unless he thought that he had a serious problem that justified such expenditure.[70]

---

[67]   R. J. Wosnitzer and A. J. Bridges (2007), *Aggression and Sexual Behavior in Best-Selling Pornography: A Content Analysis Update*. Paper presented at the 57th Annual Meeting of the International Communication Association, San Francisco, Calif.

[68]   K. Doran, "Industry Size, Measurements, and Social Costs," in *The Social Costs of Pornography: A Collection of Papers* (Princeton, N.J.: Witherspoon Institute, 2010).

[69]   Ibid.

[70]   Ibid.

FINDING SEVEN

≋

*Pornography consumption is philosophically
and morally problematic.*

Although this statement concentrates on the empirically measurable toll of
pornography, the use of pornography also raises philosophical questions.

The prevailing justification for pornography in our time appears to be
philosophical libertarianism. Many people regard pornography as a private
matter that does not affect others, as long as both the producers and the
consumers are consenting adults. If pressed upon the point that pornography
obviously causes harm in some families and marriages and relationships,
many people would further respond that such may be true, but beside the
point; what is most important is that people have a "right" to it. This response
is illogical. No one would argue that tobacco is not a serious public health
problem because many smokers, including lifelong smokers, do not die of
lung cancer. Likewise, the fact that not everyone becomes dependent upon
or addicted to pornography is irrelevant to the fact that pornography causes
substantial harm.

**SOME THINGS ARE SIMPLY WRONG IN PRINCIPLE, REGARDLESS
OF WHETHER PARTICULAR HARM IS DEMONSTRATED.**

Prostitution has been stigmatized and regarded as wrong in many societies
for centuries. Yet that stigmatization is not typically justified by appeal to the
immediate consequences of prostitution, but rather on the understanding
that it is intrinsically wrong. Likewise, as one writer remarked, it may be
"exceedingly difficult or impossible to map a causal link between any version
of pornography and particular harms suffered by particular women,"[71] but
that would not efface the wrong in principle constituted by pornography

---

[71]   H. Arkes, "Pornography: Settling the Question in Principle," in *The Social Costs of Pornography:
A Collection of Papers* (Princeton, N.J.: Witherspoon Institute, 2010).

nor deny the tendency of pornography to produce real harms on a vast scale.

We are reminded, rather, that material harms are not always the most decisive ground for the law. Some of the most important parts of our laws could not be justified if they had to hinge on a proof of material injuries. It was not the evidence showing harms done to the black children segregated in public schools in *Brown v. Board of Education* that made that case a landmark, but the recognition that they had been treated according to the maxims of an unjust principle. Similarly, in the regulation of speech, the law has long recognized a class of publications that are libelous per se: they can be judged as wrongful in their character and tendency quite apart from the question of whether it could be shown that any particular person has suffered a material harm as a result of these publications. The laws that in the past barred the defamation of racial groups bore that same quality. There was something wrong with denigrating a whole class of people based on race, regardless of whether one could prove a connection between any publication and a harm suffered later by any member of the race denigrated in this way.

The question of pornography has to turn then, in the same way, on the question of what is wrong about pornography in point of principle. "Pornography" came from the Greek *pornos graphos*, writing about prostitutes, and the aversion to pornography in principle leads to the ground of holding pornography to be something in principle wrong, quite apart from the harms that may be measured from time to time. The objection to pornography, rather like the objection to prostitution, "finds its proper ground in the recognition that there is something of inescapable moral significance about sex in creatures who have moral reasons for extending or withdrawing their love."[72]

Likewise, the consumption of pornography can do worse than alter the physical health of individuals. It "[destroys] the capacity for loving sexual relations,"

---

[72]   Ibid.

and therefore "is one of the great social diseases," which "is looked on with dismay by the majority—including a majority of those who are addicted to it."[73]

The signatories do not intend here to define the precise vices and sins with which pornography has traditionally been associated in various traditions. It bears noting, however, that no known society in history has taken as laissez-faire a view of pornography as many in America and parts of Western Europe do today. On the contrary, throughout history this phenomenon has more often than not been stigmatized and circumscribed by law and custom.

---

[73] See R. Scruton, "Pornography and the Courts," *Public Discourse: Ethics, Law, and the Common Good*, February 9, 2009; available at http://www.thepublicdiscourse.com/2009/02/90. For an in-depth treatment, see Scruton (2010).

FINDING EIGHT

≋

The fact that not everyone is harmed by pornography
does not entail that pornography should not be regulated.

Pornography and obscenity have historically been subject to regulation of all
kinds by localities, states, and the federal government, by appeal to a number
of legal concepts (endangerment, public decency, and harm, among them).[74]
Pornography has been opposed and condemned from various religious and
ideological perspectives, ranging from Christian moral theology to feminism.
As recently as the 1980s, feminists and conservatives convinced the Meese
Commission not only to revise earlier findings on pornography on the basis
of new science but to incorporate the feminist perspective that pornography
is discriminatory against women.[75]

Nevertheless, a series of recent federal court decisions has made it harder to
prosecute perpetrators under existing obscenity statutes. Since the middle of
the twentieth century, the First Amendment has frequently been interpreted
to protect material that the law once suppressed as obscene or pornographic.
During the 1980s, ordinances in Minneapolis and Indianapolis drafted by a
feminist professor and aimed at the regulation of pornography were struck
down in federal courts that found the prohibition of pornography to run afoul
of the First Amendment. Even though the fact of harm was not denied, the
right of free speech was judged to be more important.[76]

Yet these precedents do not preclude all legal strategies in the effort to
ameliorate the problems of pornography. It remains sound First Amendment

---

[74]　For a fuller treatment of the issues described in this section, see G. V. Bradley, "The Moral
Basis for Legal Regulation of Pornography," and J. R. Stoner, Jr., "Freedom, Virtue, and the Politics
of Regulating Pornography," in *The Social Costs of Pornography: A Collection of Papers* (Princeton,
N.J.: Witherspoon Institute, 2010).

[75]　Stoner (2010).

[76]　See also D. A. Downs, *The New Politics of Pornography* (Chicago: University of Chicago Press,
1989), for a detailed account of these events.

doctrine that truly obscene material is not protected by the Constitution, and that even legally protected materials can be regulated as to the time, place, and manner of their distribution and use. Further, the courts could reverse their precedents if faced with cases that force them to confront the emerging evidence about pornography consumption and its effects. Apart from legal means, one could reduce pornography by reducing or eliminating the profits that have created the industry. New policy ideas are necessary to combat the widespread availability of pornography, which we now know to be so harmful to society.

RECOMMENDATIONS

The signatories believe a multifaceted approach is required to reduce the social harms of current levels of pornography consumption. Such an approach was used in changing public expectations and information about tobacco over the course of the decades since 1964. They do not individually wholly endorse each particular recommendation below—they are a heterogeneous group—but they do present them as guidelines for the kinds of initiatives they believe to be desirable in view of the evidence discussed.

THE THERAPEUTIC COMMUNITY, which possesses considerable empirical evidence about the harms of internet pornography consumption, should take the lead both in amassing new evidence and in disseminating that evidence at the highest levels of public opinion and governance.

First, as a corollary, the signatories invoke the principle *first, do no harm.* Many therapists today are ignorant of the scale of pornography use in America and of the statistics mentioned throughout this statement testifying to its manifold harms. Many have uncritically accepted the prevailing view of pornography as anodyne entertainment, much like video games and online games.

For reasons demonstrated at length in this statement, the signatories disagree. At a minimum, *en route* to efforts to align therapeutic opinion with the empirical evidence, we urge those therapists who actually encourage the use of pornography in their counseling to couples as a "marital aid" to cease this practice. In light of the evidence of pornography's destructiveness to personal relationships, especially, we view such inappropriate therapeutic use of pornography as similar to the free distribution of tobacco to troops by the Red Cross.

Second, the signatories recommend to the therapeutic community several pressing areas of future research suggested by the empirical record as it stands: the relationship between pornography and prostitution; the factors that heighten risk for dependency and addiction; the effects on children and adolescents of exposure to pornography.

EDUCATORS AND OTHER TEACHERS should be attentive to ongoing research into the effects of pornography consumption and incorporate those findings into their curricula as appropriate. This is particularly urgent, in our view, for those teachers and other leaders involved with pre-adolescents, as significant pornography consumption by adolescent boys in particular is a growing phenomenon. Sexual education programs, for example, should include a component about pornography and the sex industry so that young people understand the underpinnings and implications of the commercialization of sex, and the impact of pornography on those who use it and those involved in its production.

JOURNALISTS, EDITORS, BLOGGERS, and others influential in forming public opinion are similarly called upon to lead in the investigation of pornography's effects. Investigative journalists, for example, might examine the relationship between the industry and its lobbying and financial influence. Factual, non-sensationalized accounts of how and why "actors" are drawn to the industry are much needed.

Also needed are accounts of the links between human trafficking and the pornography industry. Through such examinations, the field of journalism would contribute much-needed information to the lay public, many of whom remain considerably more ignorant about the actual effects of pornography production, consumption, dependence, and addiction than are those in the therapeutic community.

PRIVATE INDUSTRY can also take the lead in ameliorating some of the harm caused by pornography addiction and dependence.

First, corporations ought to implement policies in the workplace that make clear there is no tolerance for pornography and sexual exploitation. But they also need to take an enlightened view of the employee who has developed a pornography problem that jeopardizes his or her job, and help that person break the habit rather than simply firing him or her. Many corporations and insurance companies now encourage an employee who has developed an alcohol or substance-abuse problem to seek appropriate counseling, on the mutual understanding that the employee has developed an addiction beyond his or her control, and that it will benefit both the company and the employee to be in partnership in breaking that addiction.

Second, the hospitality industry in particular is called upon here to be mindful of its responsibilities to society. Many people first encounter pornography on television in a hotel room. Some hotels already block content on their televisions in the interest of protecting those who do not want their space invaded with pornographic imagery, but others tempt their patrons by advertising access to pornography and providing pay-per-view pornographic films.

POPULAR CULTURE AND CELEBRITIES are called upon to use the bully pulpit conferred by their celebrity status to discourage the glamorization of pornography and the enabling view that "everybody does it." Just as Hollywood has taken the lead in discouraging tobacco addiction by de-glamorizing the depiction of smoking over the years, so could progressively minded entertainers and other industry members use their unprecedented reach into the lives of young people, especially, to back away from the current glamorization of pornography. This appeal has particular urgency in the community of popular music, where videos now routinely feature degrading, quasi-pornographic, and pornographic imagery.

In a similar vein, a public service campaign in which celebrities and others influential with young people take issue with today's "so-what" attitude toward pornography would be especially helpful. Such a campaign could speak out against pornified images of women, against the acceptance of stripper culture, and against the mainstreaming of pornography in juvenile culture.

GOVERNMENT ON VARIOUS LEVELS can play a vigorous role in reducing the costs to society of pornography consumption, and accordingly the signatories offer these recommendations:

First, the government should legislate to make pornography no more legal on standard servers used by ordinary people than it is in the mail. Some suggest that it could be a condition of operating an internet server that service is not offered to sites that propagate obscenity. Others, including some of the signatories to this statement, object to liability rules that would require those who operate servers to police them, preferring instead direct penalties for those who produce or distribute obscene material. As a first step, in the United States, sites targeted for enforcement could be defined as those that make available material deemed obscene even under current First Amendment law: that "appeals to the prurient interest in sex; portrays, in a patently offensive way, sexual conduct specifically defined by applicable state law; and, taken as a whole, does not have serious literary, artistic, political, or scientific value" (*Miller v. California*).

Second, and as a corollary, political leaders should use the bully pulpit for a public campaign to show that pornography—even when it does not satisfy the narrow, legal definition of "obscene"—is not necessarily "speech" as protected by the First Amendment. Despite the current judicial atmosphere in which the First Amendment typically is invoked to trump most other considerations, the fact remains that rights can be limited if their exercise causes demonstrable harm to others. Such is the meaning of Justice Oliver Wendell Holmes, Jr.'s famous observation that one does not have the right falsely to yell "fire!" in a crowded theater.

It is our contention that the reflexive protection of pornography on First Amendment grounds will become increasingly unsustainable as the harms caused by today's consumption become an increasing part of the public store of knowledge—an effort to which the signatories hope this statement contributes.

Third, in a similar vein, all "adult" material (print and digital) should carry a warning about the addictive potential of pornography and consequent possible psychological harm to the consumer.

Fourth, the Department of Justice unit dedicated to the prosecution of obscenity needs to be redeveloped and redeployed to address the specific and multifaceted phenomenon of internet pornography.

AND FINALLY, legislatures are called upon to create a new, private (civil, not criminal) right of action, called the "negligent exposure of a minor or an unwilling adult to obscene materials."[77] This civil action would expand upon existing laws against endangering the welfare of children and would permit recovery for emotional offense to adults.[78]

---

[77]   "Obscenity" is here defined by the standard articulated in *Miller v. California*, 1973: "works which, taken as a whole, appeal to the prurient interest in sex, which portray sexual conduct in a patently offensive way and which, taken as a whole, do not have serious literary, artistic, political, or scientific value."

[78]   For more details on how such an initiative might work, see G. V. Bradley, "The Moral Basis for Legal Regulation of Pornography," in *The Social Costs of Pornography: A Collection of Papers* (Princeton, N.J.: Witherspoon Institute, 2010).

CONCLUSIONS

As noted throughout this statement, the famous 1964 Surgeon General's report on tobacco consumption is in many ways the inspiration and public health model for this project. That 1964 Report summarized the evidence of its time as follows: "cigarette smoking is a hazard of sufficient importance in the United States to warrant appropriate remedial action."

Likewise, the consumption of internet pornography on today's scale is a social and personal health hazard of sufficient importance in the United States to warrant appropriate remedial action, including but not limited to the suggested recommendations of this statement.

The triad of pornography consumption, dependency, and addiction is clearly not the only problem facing our society. However, it is a serious problem as well as an under-recognized one, which is why the signatories urge readers of all beliefs and political persuasions to attend to the empirical record of its harms. Those who would ignore that record do so to the detriment of the society it is shaping, not only for the adults among us, but for those others who surely deserve to become adults in a world less glutted by pornographic imagery.

SIGNATORIES

Hadley Arkes
Edward N. Nay Professor of Jurisprudence and American Institutions
Amherst College

Francis J. Beckwith
Professor of Philosophy and Church-State Studies
Baylor University

Gerard V. Bradley
Professor of Law
University of Notre Dame Law School

Margaret F. Brinig
Fritz Duda Family Professor of Law
University of Notre Dame Law School

J. Budziszewski
Professor of Government and Philosophy
University of Texas, Austin

James W. Ceaser
Professor of Politics
University of Virginia

Sharon W. Cooper, MD
Adjunct Professor, Department of Pediatrics
University of North Carolina, Chapel Hill School of Medicine
Consultant, National Center for Missing and Exploited Children

Jeffrey Dew
Assistant Professor of Family, Consumer, and Human Development
Utah State University

Kirk Doran
Bradley Visiting Fellow
The Witherspoon Institute

Mary Eberstadt
Research Fellow
The Hoover Institution

Jean Bethke Elshtain
Laura Spelman Rockefeller Professor of Social and Political Ethics
University of Chicago

Michael O. Emerson
Allyn R. and Gladys M. Cline Professor of Sociology
Rice University

John M. Finnis
Professor of Law and Legal Philosophy
Oxford University

Robert P. George
McCormick Professor of Jurisprudence
Princeton University

Norval Glenn
Ashbel Smith Professor of Sociology
Stiles Professor in American Studies
University of Texas, Austin

John Haldane
Professor of Philosophy, and Director for the Centre for Ethics,
Philosophy and Public Affairs
University of St. Andrews

Donna M. Hughes
Professor and Eleanor M. and Oscar M. Carlson Endowed Chair
Women's Studies Program
University of Rhode Island

William B. Hurlbut
Consulting Professor at the Neuroscience Institute
Stanford University Medical School

Harold James
Professor of History and International Affairs
Princeton University
Marie Curie Professor
European University Institute

Byron Johnson
Professor of Sociology
Director, Program on Prosocial Behavior
Baylor University

John Keown
Rose F. Kennedy Professor of Christian Ethics
Kennedy Institute of Ethics
Georgetown University

Paul E. Kerry
Visiting Fellow, The Center for the Study of Jewish-Christian Relations
University of Cambridge

Aaron Kheriaty, MD
Assistant Professor of Psychiatry
University of California, Irvine School of Medicine

Robert D. King
Audre and Bernard Rapoport Regents Chair of Jewish Studies
and Centennial Professor of Liberal Arts
University of Texas, Austin

Robert C. Koons
Professor of Philosophy
University of Texas, Austin

Mary Anne Layden
Director, Sexual Trauma and Psychopathology Program
Center for Cognitive Therapy
Department of Psychiatry
University of Pennsylvania

Mary Graw Leary
Associate Professor
Columbia School of Law
The Catholic University of America

Joseph C. Masdeu, MD, PhD
Senior Staff Physician and Scientist
National Institutes of Health
Adjunct Professor of Neurology
New York Medical College

Wilfred M. McClay
SunTrust Bank Chair of Excellence in the Humanities
Professor of History
University of Tennessee, Chattanooga

Paul McHugh, MD
University Distinguished Service Professor of Psychiatry
Johns Hopkins University School of Medicine

Margarita Mooney
Assistant Professor of Sociology
University of North Carolina, Chapel Hill

Michael J. New
Assistant Professor of Political Science
University of Alabama

David Novak
J. Richard and Dorothy Shiff Chair of Jewish Studies
University of Toronto

Rob Palkovitz
Professor of Human Development and Family Studies
University of Delaware

Eduardo M. Peñalver
Professor of Law
Cornell Law School

Thomas Pink
Professor of Philosophy
King's College, London

Joseph Price
Assistant Professor of Economics
Brigham Young University

Alexander R. Pruss
Associate Professor of Philosophy
Baylor University

Mark Regnerus
Associate Professor of Sociology
University of Texas, Austin

Michael Reynolds
Assistant Professor in Near Eastern Studies
Princeton University

Daniel N. Robinson
Philosophy Faculty
Oxford University

Francisco Javier Romero, MD, PhD
Professor of Physiology
Dean of the Health Sciences Faculty
Universidad CEU Cardenal Herrera
Valencia, Spain

Roger Scruton
Senior Research Fellow
Blackfriars Hall
Oxford University

Thomas K. Seung
Jesse H. Jones Regents Professor in Liberal Arts
University of Texas, Austin

Betsy Page Sigman
Professor of the Practice
McDonough School of Business
Georgetown University

James R. Stoner, Jr.
Professor of Political Science
Louisiana State University

Eleonore Stump
Robert J. Henle Professor of Philosophy
St. Louis University

Gladys M. Sweeney
Academic Dean
Institute for the Psychological Sciences

Christopher Tollefsen
Professor of Philosophy
University of South Carolina

David L. Tubbs
Assistant Professor of Politics
King's College, New York

Paul C. Vitz
Emeritus Professor of Psychology
New York University
Senior Scholar
Institute for the Psychological Sciences

Candace Vogler
Professor of Philosophy
University of Chicago

Lynn D. Wardle
Bruce C. Hafen Professor of Law
J. Reuben Clark Law School
Brigham Young University

W. Bradford Wilcox
Associate Professor of Sociology
University of Virginia